THE GOD IN YOU BIBLE STUDY SERIES

CELEBRATE!
EXALTING GOD IN
PRAISE AND WORSHIP

A Bible Study by

Churches Alive!

MINISTERING TO THE CHURCHES OF THE WORLD
600 Meridian Avenue, Suite 200
San Jose, California 95126-3427

Published by

BRINGING TRUTH TO LIFE
NavPress Publishing Group
P.O. Box 35001, Colorado Springs, Colorado 80935

© 1994 by Churches Alive International
All rights reserved. No part of this publication
    may be reproduced in any form without
    written permission from NavPress, P.O.
    Box 35001, Colorado Springs, CO 80935.
ISBN 08910-90967

Cover illustration: Catherine Kanner
Inside illustrations: Rob Portlock

Unless otherwise identified, all Scripture quotations in this publication are taken from the
*HOLY BIBLE: NEW INTERNATIONAL VER-
SION*® (NIV®). Copyright © 1973, 1978, 1984
by International Bible Society. Used by permis-
sion of Zondervan Publishing House. All rights
reserved.

Printed in the United States of America

Because we share kindred aims for helping local churches fulfill Christ's Great Commission to "go and make disciples," NavPress and Churches Alive have joined efforts on certain strategic publishing projects that are intended to bring effective disciplemaking resources into the service of the local church.

For more than a decade, Churches Alive has teamed up with churches of all denominations to establish vigorous disciplemaking ministries. At the same time, NavPress has focused on publishing Bible studies, books, and other resources that have grown out of The Navigators' fifty years of disciplemaking experience.

Now, together, we're working to offer special products like this one that are designed to stimulate a deeper, more fruitful commitment to Christ in the local gatherings of His Church.

The GOD IN YOU Bible Study Series *was written by Russ Korth, Ron Wormser, Jr., and Ron Wormser, Sr., of Churches Alive. Many individuals from both Churches Alive and NavPress contributed greatly in bringing this project to publication.*

Contents

About the Author

In your hand you have just one item of a *wide range* of discipling helps, authored and developed by Churches Alive with *one overall, church-centered, biblical concept* in mind: GROWING BY DISCIPLING!

Convinced that the local church is the heart of God's plan for the world, a number of Christian leaders joined in 1973 to form Churches Alive. They saw the need for someone to work hand-in-hand with local churches to help them develop fruitful discipleship ministries.

Today, the ministry of Churches Alive has grown to include personal consulting assistance to church leaders, a variety of discipleship books and materials, and training conferences for clergy and laypeople. These methods and materials have proven effective in churches large and small of over 45 denominations.

From their commitment and experience in church ministry, Churches Alive developed the Growing by Discipling plan to help you

- minister to people at their levels of maturity.
- equip people for ministry.
- generate mature leaders.
- perpetuate quality.
- balance growth and outreach.

Every part of Growing by Discipling works together in harmony to meet the diverse needs of people — from veteran church members to the newly awakened in Christ. This discipling approach allows you to integrate present fruitful ministries and create additional ones through the new leaders you develop.

This concept follows Christ's disciplemaking example by helping you to meet people at their points of need. Then, you help them build their dependence on God so they experience His love and power. Finally, you equip them to reach out to others in a loving, effective, and balanced ministry of evangelism and helping hands.

Headquartered in San Bernardino, California, with staff across the United States and in Europe, Churches Alive continues to expand its Ministry in North America and overseas.

Introduction

We are born helpless. We can't feed, clothe, or protect ourselves. As children, we express our lack of power by saying, "When I get big I'm going to . . ." When we achieve adulthood we discover, "You can't fight city hall." In retirement, a sense of helplessness causes us to wish, "If only I were young again."

But you are not helpless. God living in you means you have power. And a sense of helplessness may be the most important factor in releasing that power in your life. Helplessness can cause you to rely solely upon God and His strength, enabling you to overcome adversaries, sin, the Devil, and life's trials.

Don't be deceived; though it is God's power in you, you must take up your armor—the Scriptures, prayer, and faith. Then, by the Holy Spirit and through cooperation with others, you'll find strength to testify and to persevere.

HOW TO USE THIS BIBLE STUDY. This book leads you through a unique approach to making the Bible meaningful. In each chapter you will study one passage, not isolated verses, to explore some of the major themes of God's Word. In the process, you'll learn Bible study methods that will be useful for the rest of your life.

You will gain maximum benefit from this book by completing the questions about the study passage and then meeting with a group of people to discuss what you discovered in your study.

No doubt, your group could spend many weeks exploring the richness of just one of these Bible passages. But much greater profit accompanies a pace of one chapter each week. This stride guarantees sustained enthusiasm that will leave people wanting more.

The leader's guide designed for this series aids the group leader in launching and guiding the discussion. It provides help for using the series in a home-study group or a classroom setting.

HINTS TO ENHANCE YOUR EXPERIENCE. The translation used in writing this study is the *New International Version* (NIV) of the Bible. All quotations are from this translation.

Though written using the NIV, this workbook adapts readily to other Bible translations. In fact, it adds interest and variety in group discussions when people use different translations.

Your book includes space to answer each question. But some people choose to mark some of their answers in an inexpensive Bible. Creating a study Bible like this allows a person to benefit from notes and information year after year.

Above all, *use* the insight you gain. The truths of the Bible were not recorded to rest on dusty shelves. God designed them to live in the experiences of people. In preparing this series, the authors never intended merely to increase your intellectual knowledge of the Bible—but to help you put into action the tremendous resources available in Jesus Christ.

"Maybe he just spilled some paint."

1.
For He Is Creator

Study Passage: Psalm 104

Focus: Psalm 104:24: How many are your works, O LORD! In wisdom you made them all; the earth is full of your creatures.

---

1 In verses 2-6, the psalmist uses several figures of speech to describe how God made the earth, separating dry land from water. What impression of God do you get from this description?

2 The psalmist also talks of how God manages His creation. List at least five statements from Psalm 104 about how God manages the world.

3 From this psalm, how would you say God feels about the things and animals He has made?

4 We have more information about the vastness of the universe than David had. To envision the immensity of God's creation, look at a single crystal of salt. Assuming it is about 1/1000 of an inch, a BB placed a foot away would represent the approximate size and distance of our sun. Continuing this model, the closest star other than our sun would have to be placed ten miles away.
   As you consider this model, how do you feel about God?

What do you want to tell Him?

How do you feel about yourself?

5 Take a twenty-minute nature walk. Look at big, small, and medium. Record what you see in each of these categories.

- The beauty of God's creation

- The power of God's creation

- The wonder of God's creation

6 In verses 31-35, the psalmist tells how he responds to these thoughts about God as Creator. How would you restate his response in your own words?

7 Why does thinking about God as Creator lead us into worship?

8 Take a minute to praise God for something He has made.

To see the world in a grain of sand,
And a heaven in a wild flower,
Hold infinity in the palm of your hand,
And eternity in an hour.

William Blake (1759–1827)

"What could be bigger than the whole world?"

2.
For He Is Majestic

Study Passage: Psalm 18

Focus: Psalm 18:31: For who is God besides the LORD? And who is the Rock except our God?

1 What are some things that cause you to sense God's greatness?

2 How does David describe God in verses 7-15 of this psalm?

How would it feel to be the object of this kind of wrath?

3 God did this to David's enemies in response to David's cry for help (verses 16-19). How does it feel to have a God like this looking out for you?

David says God takes care of him because he is *righteous* and *blameless* (verses 20-24). These words don't mean David thinks he's sinless. They mean David is committed to living with integrity and avoiding sin, and is dealing with his sin before God. (Later in his life, David committed adultery and murder, among other sins, and God still kept coming to his rescue when he dealt with his sin.)

4 Why would having a clear conscience like this be so important in entering worship?

Do verses 20-24 prick your conscience? If so, in what areas?

---

5 Three times David describes God as a Rock (verses 2,31,46). What do you think this image means?

---

6 List five things David says God does for him.

He armed David with strength for battle.

Choose one of those items you just listed, and tell how God does this for you.

God gives me the strength to fight against the temptation to worry about my future.

Restate your answer as a sentence of praise to God.

You have strengthened me with faith, and worry cannot conquer me.

7 Why do you suppose thinking about God's majesty makes David feel he can overcome the obstacles he faces?

Worship is transcendent wonder.

Thomas Carlyle (1795–1881)

If God wasn't holy.

3.
For He Is Holy

Study Passage: 1 Chronicles 16:8-36

Focus: 1 Chronicles 16:29: Ascribe to the LORD the glory due his name. Bring an offering and come before him; worship the LORD in the splendor of his holiness.

Holiness means utter separation from anything sinful or morally impure. God's holiness means He is the standard by which moral perfection or imperfection may be measured.

1 What other connotations or implications does the word *holy* have for you?

2 Read through the study passage, and list at least three
 expressions that stimulate you to worship God for His
holiness.

David said, "Glory in his holy name" (verse 10). "Name" as
used here means more than just what people are called to
distinguish one from the other. It includes all the person is in
character, authority, position, majesty, excellence, and anything else implied by the name.

3 What are your thoughts and/or feelings when you consider God's holy character, authority, position, majesty,
and excellence?

Restate these feelings in a sentence of worship to God.

4 In verse 29 we are encouraged to bring an offering and come before Him. Typically people think of an offering in the Old Testament as an animal sacrifice or today as money. What is a different kind of offering you can use to celebrate God's holiness?

5 Verse 9 says to tell of His wonderful acts. What is one of God's . . .

wonderful acts for all people?

wonderful acts for you personally?

6 What is one way telling about these wonderful acts could be incorporated into worshiping God?

7 Verse 29 says we are to "worship the LORD in the splendor of his holiness." If you close your eyes, how do you envision the splendor of his holiness?

8 In what sense do you think we should tremble before God as stated in verse 30?

9 In verses 8 and 34 David says to give thanks to God. List ten things you would like to thank Him for.

How would you suggest thanksgiving be incorporated into a worship service?

Holy, holy, holy is the Lord!
Sing, O ye people, gladly adore Him;
Let the mountains tremble at His word,
Let the hills be joyful before Him;
Mighty in wisdom, boundless in mercy,
Great is Jehovah, King over all.

"Holy Is the Lord" by Fanny J. Crosby

Getting what you want is what Christmas is all about.

4.
The Incarnation

Study Passage: Luke 1:39-80

Focus: Luke 1:68: Praise be to the Lord, the God of Israel, because he has come and has redeemed his people.

1 In chapters 1 and 2 of *Jesus!* you studied the Incarnation from earthly and heavenly perspectives. From what you already know about the Incarnation, what reasons are there for celebrating it with praise and worship?

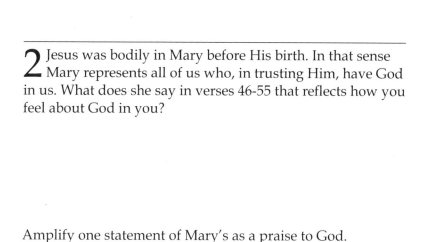

2 Jesus was bodily in Mary before His birth. In that sense Mary represents all of us who, in trusting Him, have God in us. What does she say in verses 46-55 that reflects how you feel about God in you?

Amplify one statement of Mary's as a praise to God.

3 What are some of the things you value about Christmas?

The carol "O Holy Night" speaks of the holiness of Christmas. In what way is Christmas holy?

What is one Christmas carol you think is a good song of praise and worship?

4 Zechariah was struck dumb because he did not believe God's good news regarding his future son, John the Baptist (Luke 1:18-22). As you read the events surrounding the birth of John in verses 57-66, relive these events, looking through the eyes of either Elizabeth, Zechariah, or a relative or neighbor.

What emotions do you imagine this person felt?

If you were this person, what would stir you to praise God?

5 What reasons to praise God for the Incarnation do you see in Zechariah's song? (Verses 68-79)

6 How are Mary's and Zechariah's songs similar to the psalms you studied in chapters 1 through 3 of this guide?

What recurring themes do you see in these models of praise and worship?

How can you follow these examples in your worship?

---

7 The births of Jesus and John were occasions of celebration, praise, and worship. How can you incorporate these elements into births today in a meaningful way?

In the beginning the Word existed;
and the Word was face to face with God;
yea, the Word was God Himself.
So the Word became human and lived a little
while among us, and we actually saw His glory,
and the glory of One who is an only Son
from His Father, and He was full
of spiritual blessing and truth.

John 1:1,14; The New Testament
by Charles B. Williams
(Moody Press, 1957)

5.
The Cross

Study Passage: 1 Corinthians 11:17-34

Focus: 1 Corinthians 11:26: For whenever you eat this bread and drink this cup, you proclaim the Lord's death until he comes.

1 Why does celebrating the Lord's Supper have a special place in worship? Give both universal reasons and personal reasons.

2 Paul says the Corinthians' meetings were doing more harm than good (verse 17). What was wrong with their meetings?

What kinds of things happen today that cause meetings to do more harm than good?

3 Paul cites the issue of divisions in verses 18-19. What kinds of divisions harm worship?

4 The Lord's Supper reminds us of the broken body and spilled blood. These reminders of the pain of the cross don't seem like causes for celebration and joy. What aspects of Christ's sacrifice on the cross are cause for celebration and rejoicing?

5 Paul sternly warns against partaking of the Lord's Supper in an unworthy manner. What would you consider to be an unworthy manner that might be practiced today?

6 What makes the Lord's Supper a meaningful time of worship for you?

What inhibits (or perhaps threatens to inhibit) the quality of this worship for you?

7 Hebrews 2:14 says that in dying on the cross, Jesus destroyed the devil. What are some of the other things He accomplished by His death? List as many things as you can.

Reword your list as a psalm to God by addressing each accomplishment to Him.

You destroyed the devil. You annihilated his power. You crushed his head. You put Satan under your heel.

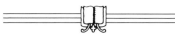

Jesus has said very clearly:
I am the love to be loved
I am the life to be lived
I am the joy to be shared
I am the bread to be eaten
I am the blood to be drunk
I am the truth to be told
I am the light to be lit
I am the peace to be given.
Jesus is everything.

Mother Teresa
Words to Live By
(Ave Maria Press, 1983)

"I'm sure this is where we buried Him."

6.
The Resurrection

Study Passage: 1 Corinthians 15

Focus: 1 Corinthians 15:57: Thanks be to God! He gives us the victory through our Lord Jesus Christ.

1 What are the issues that are of "first importance" according to verse 3?

Why are these so important?

What evidence is there that Jesus did in fact rise from the dead?

2 Some people argue that Jesus could not have risen from the dead. If they are right, what would this imply about our faith, our future, and so on? (Use arguments from the study passage and your own logic.)

3 Paul makes an analogy between a plant such as wheat and a resurrected body in verses 35-38. What is his point?

He further develops this analogy in verses 42-44. What are the four descriptions of the seed that is sown and the four descriptions of the plant that grows from that seed?

Seed Sown	Plant that Grows

Why should these truths motivate you to celebrate the resurrection of Jesus Christ?

4 Why do you think death is called the last enemy in verse 26?

What is our victory over death?

What do you think would be an appropriate way to celebrate this victory in worship as part of a funeral service?

5 The passage concludes (verses 50-58) with an anthem-like declaration of joyous victory. What feelings do you experience when you read these verses aloud? What kind of celebration do these verses bring to your mind?

6 Many of the psalms of praise contain sections rehearsing God's mighty deeds. What are some of God's mighty deeds that are part of the Resurrection?

The stone rolled back from the tomb

Reword your list of mighty deeds in the form of praise to God.

You moved the stone the guards protected, you opened the grave, you broke the seal, so Jesus could rise.

Up from the grave He arose,
With a mighty triumph over His foes;
He arose a Victor from the dark domain,
And He lives forever with His saints to reign,
He arose! He arose!
Hallelujah! Christ arose!

"Christ Arose" by Robert Lowery

"You have your way of worshiping, I have mine."

7.
By Yourself

Study Passage: Psalm 101

Focus: Psalm 101:1: I will sing of your love and justice; to you, O LORD, I will sing praise.

1 After reading Psalm 101 several times, record your thoughts regarding worshiping God by yourself. How do you feel about doing this? What makes it easy or hard for you?

2 As in Psalm 18, David speaks of "a blameless life" and "a blameless heart" (verse 2). Why do you think it is important to be blameless in your own home?

Have you thought about blamelessness since chapter 2? What are you thinking about your own blamelessness right now?

3 David says, "I will set before my eyes no vile thing" (verse 3). What are some vile things that we should not set before our eyes?

How do these things affect your worship?

Are some TV programs vile things? If you think so, list some specific programs.

4 David said he would sing of God's love and justice (verse 1). Choose one of these and amplify it by:

- Describing it more fully.

- Telling what it is like.

- Telling how it was reflected in some historical event.

- Telling how it makes you feel.

5 Summarize what David says about his relationships to others in verses 4-8.

How do your relationships affect your personal worship of God?

6 What are some things you can do when worshiping as an individual that are not easily done with others?

When is the best time of day for you to worship God?

Where is the best place for you to worship God?

---

7 Psalm 113:3 says, "From the rising of the sun to the place where it sets, the name of the LORD is to be praised." Have you ever spent an extended time in personal worship? If so tell what was good about it.

What was difficult about doing it?

---

8 David indicates that worshiping God was a daily practice for him (Psalm 145:2). Most people like variety in their daily worship to keep it from becoming a hollow ritual. What are some different ways you have spent time worshiping God?

When you pray, go into your room,
close the door and pray to your Father,
who is unseen. Then your Father,
who sees what is done in secret,
will reward you.

Matthew 6:6

"Snoring is not a joyful noise to the Lord."

8.
In the Congregation

Study Passage: Romans 15:5-13

Focus: Romans 15:7: Accept one another, then, just as Christ accepted you, in order to bring praise to God.

1 Paul implores God to grant the Romans "a spirit of unity among yourselves" (verse 5). What do you think a "spirit of unity" is?

Why is this important to congregational worship and praise?

2 What reasons for congregational worship are stated or implied in this passage?

What are other reasons can you think of for congregational worship?

What are the advantages of worshiping and praising God as a congregation?

3 Paul says believers should accept one another to bring praise to God. How do you think this acceptance should be expressed today?

What happens to worship when acceptance is lacking?

4 List the activities that are normally a part of the worship
service in your church. Rate each of the activities from
one (low) to ten (high) on how they affect your sense of worship and praise for God.

What do you think should be done when people disagree
about the significance and value of worship activities in a
congregation?

5 Approximately what portion of your church's worship
service is dedicated to praising God?

From your understanding of Scripture, what guideline
would you establish for time used for praise?

6 In verses 9-12 Paul quotes four Old Testament passages. Look up these passages in the Old Testament, and read the context of each verse quoted. What do you conclude is Paul's main point in quoting these verses?

How should this truth be applied today?

I pray and beseech you,
as many as are here present, to accompany me
with a pure heart, and humble voice,
unto the throne of the heavenly grace.

Book of Prayer of the Church of England

"Harvey is an incredible tenor."

9.
With the Heavenly Host

Study Passage: Revelation 4:1–5:14

Focus: Revelation 4:8: Day and night they never stop saying, "Holy, holy, holy is the Lord God Almighty, who was, and is, and is to come."

1 How does John describe Heaven in this passage?

What aspects of his description indicate that God is to be worshiped and praised?

2 John uses many symbolic descriptions in this passage. Choose a symbol that is meaningful to you and explain why it is so meaningful.

3 The word worship is derived from the words worth and ship (meaning quality, state, or condition). According to the study passage, of what is God worthy (be specific)? Why is He worthy?

Can you think of anything else God is worthy of, or any other reasons why He is worthy?

4 The study passage includes five different quotes of creatures worshiping God (4:8, 4:11, 5:9-10, 5:12, 5:13). Choose one of these and paraphrase the expression.

5 Make a list of all the members of the heavenly host mentioned in the study passage who are worshiping God.

How does it make you feel when you consider joining in with this heavenly host in worship of God?

6 How is Jesus Christ described in this passage?

How does John's particular view of Christ affect your praise and worship?

7 How can you incorporate the sense of worshiping with the heavenly host in your personal worship of God?

How can you incorporate the sense of worshiping with the heavenly host in your congregational worship of God?

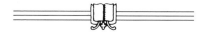

We praise thee, O God:
we acknowledge thee to be the Lord.
All the earth doth worship thee:
the Father everlasting.
To thee all Angels cry aloud:
the Heavens, and all the Powers therein.
To thee Cherubin, and Seraphin:
continually do cry,
Holy, Holy, Holy: Lord God of Sabaoth;
Heaven and earth are full of the Majesty:
of thy Glory.
The glorious company of the Apostles:
praise thee.
The goodly fellowship of the Prophets:
praise thee.
The noble army of Martyrs: praise thee.

Saint Augustine
Book of Prayer of the Church of England

"I said, 'We want prayers!'"

10.
In Prayer

Study Passage: Psalm 138

Focus: Psalm 138:2: I will bow down toward your holy temple and will praise your name for your love and your faithfulness.

---

1 Read the study passage three or four times. What mood do you think David was in when he wrote this psalm? Why?

2 In verse 1 David says he will praise God before the gods. Who do you think these gods were?

What gods exist today?

Should we praise God before these gods? Explain.

3 Different types of prayer are listed below. Tell how you think each type should be used in worship.

Thanksgiving

Intercession

Confession

Supplication

4 How does the study passage reflect David celebrating God in prayer?

5 In verse 8 David talks of God's purpose, God's love, and God's work. What is God's purpose for you? (Be as specific as possible.)

How does God's purpose relate to His love?

How does God's purpose relate to His work?

What kind of prayers dominate a person who knows God's purpose for himself or herself?

What kind of prayers dominate a person who doesn't know God's purpose?

6 What makes you want to worship God in prayer?

7 Choose a psalm that expressed your feelings toward God and offer it to Him in prayer out loud. Briefly record how this experience impacts you spiritually.

Praise is the best diet for us, after all.

Sydney Smith (1771–1845)

"Today, I'll be reading from the extra, extra large print Bible."

11.
With Truth

Study Passage: Psalm 119:97-176

Focus: Psalm 119:171-172: May my lips overflow with praise, for you teach me your decrees. May my tongue sing of your word, for all your commands are righteous.

1 Choose four verses from the study passage that link truth and worship. List the main thought from each verse.

Combine these thoughts into one central teaching.

How can this teaching be applied in worshiping God today?

2 According to Psalm 119, what are some things that happen when God's truth is not obeyed?

What can happen to worship if truth is not observed?

3 From Psalm 119, list five benefits of obeying God's Word that motivate you to praise God.

4 What ways of using God's Word in worship are most
  meaningful to you when you worship as an individual?

What ways are most meaningful when you worship in the
congregation?

5 When Jesus met the woman at the well (John 4), she
  thought one's geographical location was important in
worship. Jesus corrected this notion by saying that worship
was not restricted to "this mountain nor in Jerusalem" (John
4:21). He went on to say, "worshipers must worship in spirit
and in truth" (John 4:24). What do you think it means to worship in spirit and in truth?

What are some other things, besides geography, that some
consider important to worship but are really not important
at all?

6 When God's Word does not dominate worship, tradition, superstition, and reason usually do. What is wrong with these things dominating worship?

O Word of God incarnate,
O Wisdom from on high,
O Truth unchanged, unchanging,
O Light of our dark sky,
We praise Thee for the radiance
That from the hallowed page,
A lantern to our footsteps,
Shines on from age to age.

"O Word of God Incarnate"
by William Walsham How

Oswald's music didn't create the right atmosphere.

12.
With Music

Study Passage: Psalm 33

Focus: Psalm 33:1: Sing joyfully to the LORD, you righteous; it is fitting for the upright to praise him.

1 How do you envision the joyful singing David encourages in verse 1? Describe the picture that comes to mind.

In your experience, when have you seen people sponta-neously sing joyfully (though maybe not to the Lord)?

What do you think is the key to getting people to sing joy-fully?

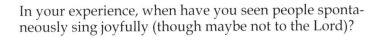

2 What two instruments are mentioned in verse 2?

What other instruments are listed in Psalm 150?

Some instruments are associated with specific moods or emotions. What mood or emotion do you associate with any of the instruments above?

Do you think it is appropriate to use instruments other than those mentioned in the Bible for worship services? Why?

3 How does David relate music to God's words and deeds in Psalm 33:1-3?

How does the psalmist relate music to God's words in Psalm 119:54?

How would you put these thoughts into practice in music today?

4 How does music affect people in general?

How does music affect you personally?

Knowing that different types of music affect people differently, what do you think would be a balanced music diet for a person?

5 Name one piece of music that particularly helps you worship God for each category below.

● God Is Creator

● God Is Majestic

● God Is Holy

● The Incarnation

● The Cross

● The Resurrection

6 How can you include music in your private worship?

7 What could be done to make the music in your congregational worship service more full of worship and praise, in your view?

Worshiping our majestic,
Holy Creator puts our whole lives into perspective.
The Incarnation, the Cross, the Resurrection,
and His continuing acts give us
more than enough reason to worship Him daily.
Keep pursuing ways to respond
to His goodness with worship.